O GOD, TERMINATE THE JOY OF MY ENEMY

DR. D. K. OLUKOYA

O GOD, TERMINATE THE JOY OF MY ENEMY
© 2012 DR. D. K. OLUKOYA
ISBN: 978-978-920-042-9
Published - November 2012 AD

Published by:
The Battle Cry Christian Ministries

322, Herbert Macaulay Street, Sabo, Yaba
P. O. Box 12272, Ikeja, Lagos
www.battlecrystore.com,
email: info@battlecrystore.com,
          customercare@battlecrystore.com,
          sales@battlecrystore.com,
Phone: 0803-304-4239, 01-8044415

I Salute my wonderful wife, Pastor Shade, for her invaluable support in the ministry.
I appreciate her unquantifiable support in the book ministry as the cover designer, art editor and art adviser.

All the scriptures are from the King James Version.

All rights reserved. Reproduction in whole or part without a written permission is prohibited. Printed in Nigeria.

Contents

CHAPTER	PAGE
1. O GOD, TERMINATE THE JOY OF MY ENEMY	4
2. DISGRACING THE ENEMY'S AGENDA	12
3. SET YOUR SPIRIT FREE	25
4. MOVING HIGHER	35
5. THE TOUCH OF FIRE	46

CHAPTER One

O God Terminate THE JOY OF MY ENEMY

Judges 16:23 says:
> Then the lords of the Philistines gathered them together for to offer a great sacrifice unto Dagon their god, and to rejoice: for they said, Our god hath delivered Samson our enemy into our hand.

In this passage we see the enemy rejoicing because Samson had been captured. I decree that your enemies will not rejoice over your life, in the name of Jesus. When Samson got into the camp of his enemies after they had captured him, he became a subject of their celebration.

PERSONAL ERRORS

Beloved, there are situations that may arise, where the enemies will be rejoicing over a person. The enemies rejoice over a person when his blood is already on their altar. If mistakenly your blood has been made available to the camp of the enemies, may be through an incision you have made, an abortion that you have done or other personal errors, it will cause the enemies to be rejoicing,

O GOD, TERMINATE THE JOY OF MY ENEMY

because they can use the blood in their hands against you anytime. I decree that by the power in the blood of Jesus if your blood is on the altar of darkness, you shall receive your deliverance, in the name of Jesus.

Another situation that may cause the enemies to be rejoicing is when they see that you are operating outside your destiny. They know what God wants you to be doing and you are not doing it but you are doing the wrong thing. They know you cannot receive divine support. The third situation under which they will be rejoicing is when they have succeeded in turning your back to God. They have succeeded in making you to do what God does not want. That is why if you are living in any known sin, it is wise to repent. Repentance is the first step in the deliverance process. If you don't repent you can do 200 deliverances and the problem will still continue.

CAPTURED BY THE ENEMY

The forth situation that makes the enemies to rejoice is when they have laid their yokes upon you. There are many people moving about now, who have invisible yokes upon their lives but they can't see them. The enemies can see them. Once that invisible yoke is there and it is not removed, the enemies will be rejoicing over the person. I pray that, every yoke of darkness upon your life today, shall be dissolved by the power of God, in the name of Jesus.

The enemies rejoice over you, when part of you is in their possession. The enemies rejoice when they notice that you have been rendered spiritually powerless and cannot fight back. I pray that if the enemies are attacking you now, pushing you to what you should not do, you shall be set free now, in the name of Jesus. The easiest position under which the enemies rejoice is when they push you into sexual immorality. Also, when the enemies see that you are carrying out their agenda, they would rejoice over you.

O GOD, TERMINATE THE JOY OF MY ENEMY

BLOOD GUILTINESS

When you have gone to the camp of the enemies for help and have not cancelled what you went there to do, they will be rejoicing. Another situation in which the enemies rejoice is when there is a blood crying against you. That is why you should not shed blood. You have to be very careful so that the blood will not cry against you. Any abortion you have done as a man or a woman, the blood certainly would be crying. You need to silence any blood speaking against you. Another position under which the enemies will be rejoicing is when you are repeating the iniquity of your father's house. The last reason I want to give you why the enemies rejoice is when you are prayerless or when your prayer carries no power or fire.

Prayer Points

1. I release myself from any ancestral demonic pollution, in the name of Jesus.
2. I release myself from any demonic pollution emanating from my parent's religion, in the name of Jesus.

3. I release myself from any demonic pollution emanating from my past involvement in any demonic religion, in the name of Jesus.
4. I break and loose myself from every idol-related association, in the name of Jesus.
5. I release myself from every dream pollution, in Jesus' name.
6. Let every satanic attack against my life in my dreams be converted to victory, in the name of Jesus.
7. Let all rivers, trees, forests, evil companions, evil pursuers, pictures of dead relatives, snakes, spirit husbands, spirit wives and masquerades manipulated against me in the dream be completely destroyed by the power in the blood of the Lord Jesus.
8. Every evil plantation in my life, I command you: **come out with all your roots, in the name of Jesus!** (*Lay your hands on your stomach and keep repeating the emphasised area.*)

9. Evil strangers in my body, come out of your hiding places, in the name of Jesus.
10. I disconnect any conscious or unconscious linkage with demonic caterers, in the name of Jesus.
11. Let all avenues of eating or drinking spiritual poisons be closed, in the name of Jesus.
12. I cough out and vomit, any food eaten from the table of the devil, in the name of Jesus. (*Cough them out and vomit them in faith. Prime the expulsion.*)
13. Let all negative materials circulating in my blood stream be flushed out, in the name of Jesus.
14. I drink the blood of Jesus. (*Physically swallow and drink it in faith, keep doing this for some time.*)
15. *Lay one hand on your head and the other on your stomach or navel and begin to pray like this*: Holy Ghost fire, burn from the top of my head to the soles of my feet. (*Begin to mention every organ of your body: your kidney, liver, intestine, blood, etc. You must not rush at this level, because the fire will actually come and you may start feeling the heat.*)
16. I cut myself off from every spirit of... (*mention the name of your place of birth*), in the name of Jesus.

17. I cut myself off from every territorial spirit and curse, in Jesus' name.
18. I cut myself off, from every family spirit and curse, in the name of Jesus.
19. Holy Ghost fire, purge my life.
20. I claim my complete deliverance, in the name of Jesus, from the spirit of... (*mention those things you do not desire in your life*).
21. I break the hold of any evil power over my life, in Jesus' name.
22. Jesus, I thank You for purging me and filling me with your revival fire.

CHAPTER Two

Disgracing the ENEMY'S AGENDA

The enemy has an evil agenda which is to imprison you in a terrible cage.

There was a fearful believer I knew. He was so fearful that every night before he went to bed, he would read at least seven psalms. Anytime he did not read those psalms and did not pray very hard, he had terrible dreams. Every little thing that went wrong in his life even if it was the falling of his shoes, he attribute it to wizards, witches, sacrifices done against him, juju, magic and voodoo. He was what we can call a Christian or spiritual crab.

There are many Christians like that called crab Christians. The crab is not a very popular animal. It doesn't take any risks.

The man never liked his mother-in-law. Because she had very big eyes and very flat feet, he believed she was a witch. One day, the Lord did something to cure the man forever. An angel of the Lord took him to a witchcraft meeting to watch and to listen. Later, the chairman of the meeting came in and the man did not recognise him. Later the assistant chairperson came in and he recognised him. She was a prophetess in his former church and had laid hands on his head several times. He wanted to cry but he remembered what the angel told him. As other people were coming in, all of a sudden, he saw his mother in-law and next to her was his own mother.

DEEP SECRETS

When the meeting started, the witches and wizards began to talk about what they were going to do and the instructions they were going to carry out. They began to discuss about Christians. Then he heard them say, "If the Christians realise how much harm they could do to evil powers, they would have finished all of us." They stated that one of their strategies was to keep the Christians from realising the power they had, and that one way they could do that easily was by caging the minds of ignorant believers.

As they kept revealing deep secrets concerning the priviledges given to the believers they made a startling revelation: "We know that God has opened doors for them. We cannot close that door, but we can prevent them from entering." At that point the meeting ended.

TERRIBLE ADVERSARIES

The brother was amazed and he understood certain things that he ought to have understood. He discovered that the door of blessings that God has opened unto His people cannot be closed by the enemies.

First Corinthians 16:9 says:

> *For a great door and effectual is opened unto me, and there are many adversaries.*

This is as strange statement coming from Paul the Apostle. There are many adversaries.

THE AGENDA

The enemies' agenda is to keep the believers from going inside their place of blessings. But they cannot shut the door, for the Bible says, "When He openenth, no man can shut the door." As children of God, we should understand that we are entitled to the best in every aspect of life. God has set before us an open door in all ramifications of life.

Let me ask you these questions:
1. What will you do if you know that you could not fail?
2. What could you do if you realise that the door you have been waiting for has been opened?

You should do what is stated below:

> *Open to me the gates of righteousness: I will go into them, and I will praise the LORD. Ps. 118:19.*

THE OBSTACLES
The devil would always put obstacles on your way. They may come in the following ways:
1. Termination in your place of work.
2. Lack of capital.

3. Lack of education.
4. Inferiority complex.
5. Continuous business failure.
6. Bad health.
7. Poor family background.

The obstacles will always be there. If they are not there, it is unlikely that it is not God that opened that door. But once the door is opened by the Almighty, there would be many adversaries whose idea is to hold you down and say, "No, you can't enter into this place." That is why it is said that the road with the least resistance will lead you nowhere.

However, as a believer, your greatest hindrances are not witches and wizards but yourself. 'You' are the greatest hindrance to what God wants to do in your life.

HOW?
1. **THOUGHTS**
   Through your thoughts, things that cross your mind regularly, things you meditate on or think about.

They may not stay in your mind for long but the enemy can use them as a springboard.

2. **IMAGINATION**
That is the picture of things that come up in your mind or that your mind is painting.

Herein lies the greatest problem of most believers.

> *For as he thinketh in his heart, so is he: Eat and drink, saith he to thee; but his heart is not with thee.* Prov. 23:7.

Your thoughts have the power to create for you what you think about. If you send out thoughts of victory, you will get victory. If you send out thoughts of success, you will get success.

THE SNARE
Fear is the wrong use of our imagination. Thoughts or imaginations shape our lives. The enemies that do not want a man to enter into the door already opened by

God would start the attack from the mind. And if they defeat you at the thought level, then they will move to your imagination. And once they defeat you there, you will be unable to enter the door opened for you by the Lord.

Thoughts and imagination are the greatest weapons of the adversaries to arrest and bring us under subjection. So, when you arrest the thoughts and imaginations, actions would not follow. It is the imagination that sponsors actions. The thoughts you are thinking are the seed you are sowing. You cannot be thinking in terms of failure and hope to succeed. You cannot be thinking of weakness and expect to be strong.

EVIL THOUGHTS

When you begin to think fear, you cannot be courageous. If you begin to think doubt you cannot have faith. So, the greatest prison yard is not the witch or wizard, but you, your thoughts and your imaginations.

O GOD, TERMINATE THE JOY OF MY ENEMY

Your body may be caged but your mind should not be caged. Our lives now are products of all our thoughts of yesterday. You become what you allow yourself to think. And the ancestor of every action we carry out is our thought.

When you have a clear and good thinking, the Lord uses it to move your life forward. Local thinking will keep you local. Restricted thinking will keep you restricted. So, what you think, greatly determines what you become.

What to do?
1. **Watch what enters your mind.** Be the immigration officer at the door of your heart.

2. **Arrest some thoughts before they gain entry.**
3. **Concentrate on the Scriptures.** Soak yourself in the word of God. Memorise your Bible.
4. Capture every bad thought and every bad imagination and replace them with the thoughts of the things of God.

Philipians 4:8 says:

> *Finally, brethren, whatsoever things are true, whatsoever things are honest, whatsoever things are just, whatsoever things are pure, whatsoever things are lovely, whatsoever things are of good report; if there be any virtue, and if there be any praise, think on these things.*

Replace evil thoughts with good thoughts. Throw evil thoughts out of your mind. Don't allow the birds of darkness, birds of evil thoughts and imagination, to take control of your heart. Don't imagine evil things against your own life. Destroy the greatest weapon which the enemy is using against your destiny.

Prayer Points

1. Let every organised strategy, of the hosts of the demonic world against my life, be rendered useless, in the name of Jesus.

2. Let every demonic influence, targeted at destroying my vision, dream and ministry, receive total disappointment, in Jesus' name.
3. Let every demonic trap set against my life be shattered into pieces, in the name of Jesus.
4. All unfriendly friends, militating against my life, receive commotion and be disorganised, in the name of Jesus.
5. Father Lord, let my life, ministry and prayer life be extremely dangerous for the kingdom of darkness, in the name of Jesus.
6. All demonically organised seductive appearances to pull me down, be rendered null and void, in the name of Jesus.
7. My Lord and my God, raise intercessors to stand in the gap for me always, in the name of Jesus.
8. I reject, all uncontrollable crying, heaviness and regrets, in the name of Jesus.
9. Father Lord, help me so that my divine spiritual assignments shall not be transferred to another person, in the name of Jesus.

10. I command all organised forces of darkness against my life, to receive commotion, lighting and thunder, in the name of Jesus.
11. All demonically organised networks against my spiritual and physical ambition, be put to shame, in the name of Jesus.
12. I command all demonic mirrors and monitoring gadgets against my spiritual life to crush into pieces, in the name of Jesus.
13. Let everything about my enemies be soaked in the blood of Jesus and in the fire of the Holy Ghost.
14. I paralyse any attempt by the devil to use any ceremony as a cover-up to carry out an evil assignment against my life, in the name of Jesus.
15. Let every evil river, emanating from the deceased be cut off and rendered ineffective, in the name of Jesus. (*This is relevant at a burial ceremony*).
16. I cover myself, my family and my vehicle with the blood of Jesus.
17. I fire back to the sender, any planned evil arrow directed against me during the ceremonies, in the name of Jesus.

18. Lord, let my body, soul and spirit be turned into hot coals of fire.
19. I paralyse and render impotent, any negative speech, invited curse and masked evil statements against me during this ceremony, in the name of Jesus.
20. Lord, take total control of my plans and activities, in the name of Jesus.
21. Father Lord, let all the food and drinks that will be served receive sanctifying power of the blood of Jesus.
22. Let your fire of protection be upon all guests, visitors and participants, in the name of Jesus.
23. Lord, let Your name alone be glorified at the end of everything.
24. I bind all evil spirits in me or that are attacking me, in Jesus' name.
25. Thank God for the victory.

CHAPTER Three

Set your SPIRIT FREE

O GOD, TERMINATE THE JOY OF MY ENEMY

Man is a sprit, living inside a body and having a soul. The greatest problem that can affect a man has to start with the spirit. Once something goes wrong with the spirit, it is just a matter of time before it begins to manifest physically. The Bible describes various states in which the spirit of a man could be imprisoned. To experience wholesomeness you must set your spirit free from the following spirit arresters.

1. **The aggrieved spirit:** This usually happens when a person is suffering rejection or experiencing pain and heat. Such a person needs comfort, the comforting oil of the Holy Spirit.

2. **The fearful or timid spirit:** Second Timothy 1:7 says:

   > *For God hath not given us the spirit of fear; but of power, and of love, and of a sound mind.*

3. **The troubled spirit:** This is when a person's spirit is in a disturbed state. For example, when anxiety, agitation, alarm or distress fill the spirit. There are so many troubled spirits like that. Everything may seem all right on the surface, but right inside, the spirit there is troubled. Many people have passed through these kind of stages. Once a spirit is in that kind of state, it will pick up all other negative things going about in the environment.

If God opens your eyes into the world of the spirit, you will see a lot of evil things in circulation, looking for whom to attach themselves to. Lay your hands on your chest now, close your eyes and pray like this: I reject, every evil attachment in the spirit, in the name of Jesus.

When I was in the university, I had a classmate who was always boasting that he did not need to read before he could pass his examinations, since he read all his books in the spiritual world. He went on to say that there was a better world under the water and that was where he went every night.

O GOD, TERMINATE THE JOY OF MY ENEMY

You may not believe it, but there is actually a fantastic world in the sea which is better than what we see here. Down there, they have a fantastic laboratory. It is from that laboratory that people bring materials for the production of most of the cosmetics you see around and there are also many satanic agents from there.

What this former classmate of mine used to do was just to allow his spirit to get out of his body and into the world of spirits. However, one day, he met some wicked spirits on the way. They got him trapped and he could not come back to his body and problem started. Everybody ran helter skelter to save his life, for even though he was breathing, he could not wake up.

A doctor who was brought to examine the body said, "I have never seen this before in medical science." However, after sometime the spirits released his spirit and it came back into his body. But he was never the same again. Wicked spirits operate in dreams; this is why we take dreams seriously. What most of us call dream is not what it is. It is rather an insight into what is going on in the spirit world. Our spirits and souls operate in the spirit world while our bodies remain where they are. If your spirit is weak and it goes into the world of the spirit and encounters some powerful spirits there, they will beat it into retreat. If you are not feeding your spirit with the word of God, if all you care for is to look after your body and apply perfumes and cosmetics, when the time of warfare comes in the spirit, that spirit that you have not fed will not be able to help you.

This is the reason why people scream for help in the dream when masquerades are running after them, because spiritually they cannot wait to fight. Your spirit may have no strength because the time you ought to be feeding it with the word of God and prayers, you are busy examining and pampering your body.

4. **The fainting spirit:** When stress is becoming too much for some people, their spirits can be overwhelmed as the psalmist says. At this stage,

they can give in to despair. Disappointments can also be used so severe some people so that it taps life out of the spirits. In such a case, a lively spirit will suddenly become weak.

People in that situation need to be revived. Now, lay your hands on your chest and sing this song with all seriousness: "Send down revival Lord. Let it start within my soul. Holy Ghost revival, pentecostal fire." Now, convert it to prayer: "Oh Lord, send down your revival and let it start within my soul, in Jesus' name."

5. **The broken spirit:** A person with a broken spirit is someone who has lost courage. His spirit has been beaten down by the enemy and needs to be revived. In this situation, what the person needs is the wine of God. Not many people know that God even has His wine. His wine is sweeter than all the wine you can ever think of.

Prayer Points

1. I tear down the stronghold of satan against my life, in the name of Jesus.
2. I smash, every plan of satan formed against me, in Jesus' name.
3. I smash the stronghold of satan formed against my body, in the name of Jesus.
4. Lord, let me be the kind of person that would please you.
5. Holy Spirit, bring all the work of resurrection and Pentecost into my life today, in the name of Jesus.
6. Every witchcraft power, I cast you into outer darkness, in the name of Jesus.
7. I confound every stubborn pursuer, in the name of Jesus.
8. I bring every power cursing my destiny into ineffectiveness, in the name of Jesus.
9. I strike every evil power siphoning my blessing with chaos and confusion, in the name of Jesus.

10. I nullify the incantations of evil spiritual consultants, in Jesus' name.
11. I turn the evil device of household witchcraft upside down, in the name of Jesus.
12. I render every local satanic weapon harmless, in the name of Jesus.
13. I receive deliverance from the spirit of anxiety, in Jesus' name.
14. I bind every spirit of mental stagnation, in the name of Jesus.
15. I release myself from the power and authority of any curse, in the name of Jesus.
16. I renounce any unholy covenants involving my life, in Jesus' name.
17. I grab, every stubborn problem and smash it against the Rock of salvation, in the name of Jesus.
18. I nullify, every sacrifice offered to demons against me, in Jesus' name.
19. Every power, cursing my destiny, be silenced, in the name of Jesus.
20. I break the power of any incense burnt against me, in Jesus' name.

21. Every python spirit, go into the hot desert and be burnt, in the name of Jesus.
22. Let the blood of Jesus poison the roots of all my problems, in the name of Jesus.
23. I go back to Adam and Eve on both sides of my bloodline, and I cut down every evil root, in the name of Jesus.
24. I reverse every improper operation of my body organs, in Jesus' name.
25. Every evil contract working against my life, be re-written by the blood of Jesus.
26. I reverse every satanic calendar for my life, in the name of Jesus.
27. Anything my ancestors have done, to pollute my life, be dismantled now, in the name of Jesus.
28. I refuse to be in the right place at the wrong time, in Jesus' name.
29. I bind every negative energy in the air, water and ground working against me, in the name of Jesus.
30. Anything from the kingdom of darkness that has made it its business to hinder me:

a. I single you out right now and bind you, in the name of Jesus.
b. Be bound with chains that cannot be broken, in the name of Jesus.
c. I strip off all your spiritual armour, in the name of Jesus.
d. Lose the support of other evil powers, in the name of Jesus.
e. Do not involve yourself with me again, in the name of Jesus.
31. Lord Jesus, I thank you for the victory.

CHAPTER Four

Moving HIGHER

O GOD, TERMINATE THE JOY OF MY ENEMY

The secret of spiritual power and progress is to keep burying yourself in the ocean of God's power. Those who have ever been spiritually catapulted to any reasonable height are the men and women who are filled with the Spirit of God. However, for you to drink God's wine, you will have to meet the following requirements:

1. **You must be a complete Christian:** Who is a complete Christian? He is one that is born again. He must have surrendered to God with notable changes. So many people have an erroneous impression that they are born again because they have been baptised as babies or "confirmed" in their churches. Being born again is the assurance of the Holy Spirit that you are saved, that inner conviction must be there. You are sure within you, that if God says, "Enough, my daughter," or "Enough, my son come," you will be happy going, because you are sure that you are going to meet your Father in heaven. But anytime they talk about your Father's home in heaven and something within you

say, "Do you think you are qualified for what they're talking about?" then you must check your life.

A lot of church members are not saved and it is very sad. A lot of church members are just playing religion. Many have not been transformed. All that has happened to most of them is a change of name and not a change of life. A complete Christian must have the assurance and the joy of salvation. This is important because no man can serve the Lord with all his heart unless he is sure about his salvation. The reason why some people are not happy when they are giving offering is that they are not sure of their salvation.

Thank God that at the MFM, our stand is on the word of God which says, "Let not your right hand know what your left hand is doing." We don't have tithe or offering cards here, whereby people write their names and what they are giving. It is the people who are not saved that are being forced to give to their Father's work. It is those who are not saved that ask such questions as "What do the pastors do with the offering money."

THE GREATEST GIFT

The advice is very simple: If you do not trust the pastor to give him your offering, take it to God yourself. Take a bus or an aircraft to God and say: "God, I have come to pay my tithe. You can have it." It is also when people are not saved that they look for church posts. When you have salvation you have the greatest gift of all. All other gifts become less important. If you are not careful those other things will even put your salvation in trouble. You cannot put your all into the service of the Lord, when you have some doubts in your heart whether you will get to heaven or not.

You must be a happy Christian: The joy and happiness of a Christian has nothing to do with circumstances, because at the end of the day, whether positive or negative, all circumstances will fade away. The day they say 'dust to dust, ashes to ashes," or the day the trumpet will sound, everybody will forget important. In fact, the Bible says that they shall be roasted with fire.

A complete Christian must be a happy Christian. So, if you find that you are not happy or that your happiness is tied to money, clothes, houses, etc, then you better seek a genuine salvation. If all the testimony you have to give is "I thank God, when I got into this church I was wearing bathroom slippers, but now, God has given me Italian shoes." "I came to this church with Okada without an engine, now I have Okada with engine." "Glory be to God, when I came here I had a Volkswagen beetle car, now I have a Lexus car. If these are all you have to say, check your salvation because your greatest testimony should be the salvation of your soul. All other things will end here. You can't carry them along with you. When the trumpet sounds, your wealth will not fly with you.

You must be a soul winner: Not everybody will be a preacher, but your life must be a witness to others.

When others see you, they must see the glory of God in your life. Your life should convert people, not drive them away from the Lord. We have a lot of spiritual touts who come to the house of God. All they come to do in MFM is to beg people for money. They do not want to pray to get their breakthrough, they just want to be parasites. They go to the car park and look for those who have big cars and beg them for money. People of this kind are just blocking the way to their breakthroughs.

A COMPLETE CHRISTIAN

A complete Christian must show by his life that he is a soul winner. Let me go through this again. A complete Christian must be saved and have the assurance of salvation. He must be joyful and happy. He must be a soul winner. If any of these three things are lacking he will not be able to drink the wine of God. The Bible seriously warns us not to be spiritual babies. Hebrews 6:1: *Therefore leaving the principles of the doctrine of Christ, let us go on unto perfection; not laying again the foundation of repentance from dead works, and of faith toward God.*

SPIRITUAL BABIES

Don't be a spiritual baby. Ephesians 4:14 says:

> *That we henceforth be no more children, tossed to and fro, and carried about with every wind of doctrine, by the sleight of men, and cunning craftiness, whereby they lie in wait to deceive .*

And Galatians 4:1-3 says:

> *Now I say, That the heir, as long as he is a child, differeth nothing from a servant, though he be Lord of all; But is under tutors and governors until the time appointed of the father. Even so we, when we were children, were in bondage under the elements of the world.*

We should not remain babies. God's plan under the new covenant is for every believer to be filled with the Holy Spirit. Ephesians 5:18 says:

> *And be not drunk with wine, wherein is excess; but be filled with the Spirit.*

GOD'S WINE

God's plan under the new covenant is that every believer should be drunk with the Holy Spirit and not with physical wine. The question is, have you been drunk with the Holy Spirit? According to Acts 19, Paul encouraged the Ephesians to be filled with the Holy Spirit, stressing the need for the constant filling of the Holy Spirit. So, to get catapulted spiritually, you also must continuously drink God's wine.

There is no way a Christian who prays in tongues for half an hour in the spirit before praying in English or whatever language can be compared to a believer who only prays for five minutes a day, and not in the spirit. The person praying in the spirit is charging his battery, while the other person is not doing so.

Prayer Points

1. Lord, cleanse all the soiled parts of my life. In the name of Jesus
2. Lord, refresh every dry area of my life. In the name of Jesus
3. Lord, heal every wounded part of my life. In the name of Jesus
4. Lord, bend every evil rigidity in my life. In the name of Jesus
5. Lord, re-align every satanic straying in my life. In the name of Jesus
6. Lord, let the fire of the Holy Spirit heat every satanic freeze in my life. In the name of Jesus
7. Lord, give me a life that kills death. In the name of Jesus
8. Lord, kindle in me the fire of charity. In the name of Jesus
9. Lord, glue me together where I am opposed to myself. In the name of Jesus

O GOD, TERMINATE THE JOY OF MY ENEMY

10. Lord, enrich me with Your gift. In the name of Jesus
11. Lord, quicken me and increase my desire for the things of heaven. In the name of Jesus
12. By Your rulership, O Lord, let the lust of the flesh in my life die. In the name of Jesus
13. Lord Jesus, increase daily in my life. In the name of Jesus
14. Lord Jesus, maintain your gifts in my life. In the name of Jesus
15. Lord, refine and purge my heart, in the name of Jesus.
16. Holy Spirit, inflame and fire my heart, in the name of Jesus.
17. Lord Jesus, lay your hands upon me and quench every rebellion in me.
18. Holy Ghost fire, begin to burn away every self-centredness in me, in the name of Jesus.
19. Father Lord, breathe your life-giving breath into my soul, in the name of Jesus.
20. Lord, make me ready to go to wherever You send me.
21. Lord Jesus, never let me shut You out.

22. Lord Jesus, never let me try to limit You to my capacity.
23. Lord Jesus, work freely in me and through me.
24. Lord, purify the channels of my life.
25. Let your heat, O Lord, consume my will, in the name of Jesus.
26. Let the flame of the Holy Spirit blaze upon the altar of my heart, in the name of Jesus.
27. Lord Jesus, come like blood into my veins.
28. Lord, order my spirit and fashion my life in Your will.
29. Lord, let Your fire, burn away in me all that is not holy in Your will.
30. Lord, let Your fire generate power in my life.
31. Lord Jesus, impart to me thoughts higher than my own thoughts.
32. Holy Spirit, come as dew and refresh me, in the name of Jesus.
33. Holy Spirit, guide me in the way of liberty, in the name of Jesus.
34. Holy Spirit, blow upon me so that sin would no more find place in me, in the name of Jesus.
35. Holy Spirit, where my love is cold, warm me up, in Jesus' name.

CHAPTER Five

The Touch the FIRE

To do exploits in life, you need the touch of fire. You need an encounter that will leave you with a touch of fire. Isaiah received fire from the altar of God and was no longer the same. Let us read the details of his fire encounter and glean vital lessons from his experience.

1. **Have a personal encounter with the Lord.**

You should be able to say clearly and with certainty, how and when you met God. If you cannot remember when you got born again, it is unlikely that you are. If you are not sure that you are born again, it shows that you are not. Some people say they got born again several times. It is not possible; you are either born again or you are not. A person who gives his or her life to the Lord Jesus, changes. The Bible says, "He becomes a new creature, old things are passed away and all things become new."

2. See yourself as you are.

Do not deceive yourself or compare yourself with other people. Peter had fished all night and Jesus came to tell him where to throw his net to catch fish. He did, and he caught a lot. It was then that he realised that he was a sinner. He saw himself the way he was. Do not look at the mirror of someone else to see yourself. Know who you really are. When you see the real you, you will know who you really are and God will drop His coal of fire upon your tongue and destroy the things that have been limiting His power in your life.

3. Your 'King Uzziah' must die.

Anything blocking you from seeing the Lord is a 'King Uzziah'. It is that thing which prevents you from seeing divine revelation. It is the thing that makes you so comfortable that you do not have time to pray or work for God again. It is the thing which occupies your time at the expense of your prayer life and Bible study.

Take this prayer point seriously:

- My 'King Uzziah' must die today, in the name of Jesus.

It does not make sense for anyone who says he or she wants to reign with Christ to have strange dreams, where he or she is having sexual intercourse or is being pursued or is flying. This is not God's plan for His children. Your 'King Uzziah' must die.

King Uzziah stands for pride, over-confidence, etc. Isaiah could not see anything or move forward until King Uzziah died.

The Bible says, "Walk in the spirit and you will not fulfil the desire of the flesh." You must lay down all your weapons of rebellion and give a full control to the Holy Spirit.

4. **Pray for purging:** Ask God to purge your life and purify you.

5. Allow the Holy Spirit to possess you.

This is a practical message; your tongue is either dead or alive. There is no middle camp; you have either seen the Lord or you have not. You either see yourself the way you are, or you do not see anything.

Right there, where you are, ask the Holy Spirit to shine His light upon your life and reveal every hidden sin. Every sin of pride, malice, unforgiveness, sleeping with a man or woman to whom you are not married, are signs of rebellion and until they go, not much can happen in your life.

Uzziah must die, but before that happens, you have to open your life before the Lord. Tell Him who you are; tell Him what you are thinking about; be sincere with yourself, so that God can touch you today.

It will be sad beloved, if you take this message lightly and not allow God to touch your life. There is anointing to break every yoke of sin, destroy every bondage of bad habits and remove every cataract from your spiritual eyes, so that you too can see the Lord.

When you see the Lord, your life will no longer be the same. For your eyes to see the King of kings, something must happen.

Prayer Points

1. Thank God for the revelational power of the Holy Spirit.
2. Thank God for the purifying power of the Holy Ghost.
3. I cover myself with the blood of the Lord Jesus.
4. Father, let your fire that burns away every deposit of the enemy, fall upon me, in the name of Jesus.
5. Holy Ghost, incubate me, in the name of the Lord Jesus Christ.
6. I reject, any stamp or seal placed upon me by ancestral spirits, in the name of Jesus.

7. I release myself from every negative anointing, in the name of Jesus.
8. Let every door of spiritual leakage be closed, in the name of Jesus.
9. I challenge every organ of my body with the fire of the Holy Spirit (*lay your right hand methodically on various parts of the body beginning from the head*), in the name of Jesus.
10. Let every human spirit attacking my spirit release me, in the name of Jesus.
11. I reject, every spirit of the tail, in the name of Jesus.
12. Sing the song: "Holy Ghost fire, fire fall on me."
13. Let all evil marks on my body, be burnt off .by the fire of the Holy Ghost, in the name of Jesus.
14. Let the anointing of the Holy Ghost fall upon me and break every negative yoke, in the name of Jesus.
15. Let every garment of hindrance and dirtiness be dissolved by the fire of the Holy Ghost, in the name of Jesus.
16. I command all my chained blessings to be unchained, in the name of Jesus.

17. Let all spiritual cages, inhibiting my progress, be roasted by the fire of the Holy Spirit, in Jesus' name.
18. Lord, give unto me, the spirit of revelation and wisdom in the knowledge of you.
19. Lord, make your way plain before my face on this issue.
20. Lord, remove spiritual cataract from my eyes.
21. Lord, forgive me for every false motive or thought that has ever been formed in my heart since I was born.
22. Lord, forgive me for any lie that I have ever told against any person; system or organisation.
23. Lord, deliver me from the bondage and sin of spiritual laziness.
24. Lord, open my eyes to see all I should see concerning You and myself.
25. Lord, teach me deep and secret things.

OTHER PUBLICATIONS BY DR. D. K. OLUKOYA

1. 20 Marching Orders To Fulfill Your Destiny
2. 30 Things The Anointing Can Do For You
3. 30 Poverty Destroying Keys
4. 30 Prophetic Arrows From Heaven
5. A-Z of Complete Deliverance
6. Abraham's Children in Bondage
7. Basic Prayer Patterns
8. Be Prepared
9. Bewitchment must die
10. Biblical Principles of Dream Interpretation
11. Biblical Principles of Long Life
12. Born Great, But Tied Down
13. Breaking Bad Habits
14. Breakthrough Prayers For Business Professionals
15. Bringing Down The Power of God
16. Brokenness
17. Can God Trust You?
18. Can God?
19. Command The Morning
20. Connecting to The God of Breakthroughs
21. Consecration Commitment & Loyalty
22. Contending For The Kingdom
23. Criminals In The House Of God
24. Dancers At The Gate of Death
25. Dealing With The Evil Powers of Your Father's House
26. Dealing With Tropical Demons

OTHER PUBLICATIONS BY DR. D. K. OLUKOYA

27. Dealing With Local Satanic Technology
28. Dealing With Witchcraft Barbers
29. Dealing With Unprofitable Roots
30. Dealing With Hidden Curses
31. Dealing With Destiny Vultures
32. Dealing With Satanic Exchange
33. Dealing With Destiny Thieves
34. Deliverance Of The Head
35. Deliverance of The Tongue
36. Deliverance: God's Medicine Bottle
37. Deliverance from Evil Load
38. Deliverance From Spirit Husband
39. Deliverance From The Limiting Powers
40. Deliverance From Evil Foundation
41. Deliverance of The Brain
42. Deliverance Of The Conscience
43. Deliverance By Fire
44. Destiny Clinic
45. Destroying Satanic Masks
46. Disgracing Soul Hunters
47. Divine Yellow Card
48. Divine Prescription For Your Total Immunity
49. Divine Military Training
50. Dominion Prosperity
51. Drawers Of Power From The Heavenlies
52. Evil Appetite
53. Evil Umbrella

OTHER PUBLICATIONS BY DR. D. K. OLUKOYA

54. Facing Both Ways
55. Failure In The School Of Prayer
56. Fire For Life's Journey
57. Fire for Spiritual Battles for The 21st Century Army
58. For We Wrestle ...
59. Freedom Indeed
60. Fresh Fire (Bilingual book in French)
61. God's Key To A Happy Home
62. Healing Through Prayers
63. Holiness Unto The Lord
64. Holy Fever
65. Holy Cry
66. Hour Of Decision
67. How To Obtain Personal Deliverance
68. How To Pray When Surrounded By The Enemies
69. I Am Moving Forward
70. Idols Of The Heart
71. Igniting Your Inner Fire
72. Igniting Your Inner Fire
73. Is This What They Died For?
74. Kill Your Goliath By Fire
75. Killing The Serpent of Frustration
76. Let God Answer By Fire
77. Let Fire Fall
78. Limiting God
79. Looking Unto Jesus
80. Lord, Behold Their Threatening Madness of The Heart

OTHER PUBLICATIONS BY DR. D. K. OLUKOYA

81. Making Your Way Through The Traffic Jam of Life
82. Traffic Jam of Life
83. Meat For Champions
84. Medicine For Winners
85. My Burden For The Church
86. Open Heavens Through Holy Disturbance
87. Overpowering Witchcraft
88. Passing Through The Valley of The Shadow of Death
89. Paralysing The Riders And The Horse
90. Personal Spiritual Check-Up
91. Possessing The Tongue of Fire
92. Power To Recover Your Birthright
93. Power Against Captivity
94. Power Against Coffin Spirits
95. Power Against Unclean Spirits
96. Power Against The Mystery of Wickedness
97. Power Against Destiny Quenchers
98. Power Against Dream Criminals
99. Power Against Local Wickedness
100. Power Against Marine Spirits
101. Power Against Spiritual Terrorists
102. Power To Recover Your Lost Glory
103. Power To Disgrace The Oppressors
104. Power Must Change Hands
105. Power Must Change Hands (Prayer Points from 1995-2010)
106. Power To Shut Satanic Doors
107. Power Against The Mystery of Wickedness

OTHER PUBLICATIONS BY DR. D. K. OLUKOYA

108. Power of Brokenness
109. Pray Your Way To Breakthroughs
110. Prayer To Make You Fulfill Your Divine Destiny
111. Prayer Strategies For Spinsters And Bachelors
112. Prayer Warfare Against 70 Mad Spirits
113. Prayer Is The Battle
114. Prayer To Kill Enchantment
115. Prayer Rain
116. Prayers To Destroy Diseases And Infirmities
117. Prayers For Open Heavens
118. Prayers To Move From Minimum To
119. Praying Against Foundational Poverty
120. Praying Against The Spirit Of The Valley
121. Praying In The Storm
122. Praying To Dismantle Witchcraft
123. Praying To Destroy Satanic Roadblocks
124. Principles of Conclusive Prayers
125. Principles Of Prayer
126. Raiding The House of The Strongman
127. Release From Destructive Covenants
128. Revoking Evil Decrees
129. Safeguarding Your Home
130. Satanic Diversion of the Black Race
131. Secrets of Spiritual Growth & Maturity
132. Self-Made Problems (Bilingual book in French)
133. Seventy Rules of Spiritual Warfare
134. Seventy Sermons To Preach To Your Destiny

OTHER PUBLICATIONS BY DR. D. K. OLUKOYA

135. Silencing The Birds Of Darkness
136. Slave Masters
138. Smite The Enemy And He Will Flee
139. Speaking Destruction Unto The Dark Rivers
140. Spiritual Education
141. Spiritual Growth And Maturity
142. Spiritual Warfare And The Home
143. Stop Them Before They Stop You
144. Strategic Praying
145. Strategy Of Warfare Praying
146. Students In The School Of Fear
147. Symptoms Of Witchcraft Attack
148. Taking The Battle To The Enemy's Gate
149. The Amazing Power of Faith
150. The God of Daniel (Bilingual book in French)
151. The God of Elijah (Bilingual book in French)
152. The Vagabond Spirit
153. The Unlimited God
154. The Wealth Transfer Agenda
155. The Way Of Divine Encounter
156. The Unconquerable Power
157. The Baptism of Fire
158. The Battle Against The Spirit Of Impossibility
159. The Chain Breaker
160. The Dinning Table Of Darkness
161. The Enemy Has Done This
162. The Evil Cry Of Your Family Idol

OTHER PUBLICATIONS BY DR. D. K. OLUKOYA

163. The Fire Of Revival
164. The School of Tribulation
165. The Gateway To Spiritual Power
166. The Great Deliverance
167. The Internal Stumbling Block
168. The Lord Is A Man Of War
169. The Mystery Of Mobile Curses
170. The Mystery Of The Mobile Temple
171. The Prayer Eagle
172. The University of Champions
173. The Power of Aggressive Prayer Warriors
174. The Power of Priority
175. The Tongue Trap
176. The Terrible Agenda
177. The Scale of The Almighty
178. The Hidden Viper
179. The Star In Your Sky
180. The Star Hunters
181. The Spirit Of The Crab
182. The Snake In The Power House
183. The Slow Learners
184. The University of Champions
185. The Skeleton In Your Grandfather's Cupboard
186. The Serpentine Enemies
187. The Secrets Of Greatness
188. The Seasons Of Life
189. The Pursuit Of Success

OTHER PUBLICATIONS BY DR. D. K. OLUKOYA

190. Tied Down In The Spirits
191. Too Hot To Handle
192. Turnaround Breakthrough
193. Unprofitable Foundations
194. Victory Over Your Greatest Enemies
195. Victory Over Satanic Dreams
196. Violent Prayers Against Stubborn Situations
197. War At The Edge Of Breakthroughs
198. Wasted At The Market Square of Life
199. Wasting The Wasters
200. Wealth Must Change Hands
201. What You Must Know About The House Fellowship
202. When the Battle is from Home
203. When You Need A Change
204. When The Deliverer Need Deliverance
205. When Things Get Hard
206. When You Are Knocked Down
207. When You Are Under Attack
208. When The Enemy Hides
209. When God Is Silent
210. Where Is Your Faith
211. While Men Slept
212. Woman! Thou Art Loosed.
213. Why Problems Come Back
214. Your Battle And Your Strategy
215. Your Foundation And Destiny
216. Your Mouth And Your Deliverance

OTHER PUBLICATIONS BY DR. D. K. OLUKOYA

217. Your Mouth and Your Warfare

YORUBA PUBLICATIONS
1. Adura Agbayori
2. Adura Ti Nsi Oke Ni dii
3. Ojo Adura

FRENCH PUBLICATIONS
1. Pluie De Priere
2. Espirit De Vagabondage
3. En Finir Avec Les Forces Malefiques De La Maison De Ton Pere
4. Que l'envoutement Perisse
5. Frappez l'adversaire Et Il Fuira
6. Comment Recevior La Delivrance Du Mari Et De La Femme De Nuit
7. Comment Se Delivrer Soi-meme
8. Pouvoir Contre Les Terrorites Spirituels
9. Priere De Percees Pour Les Hommes D'affaires
10. Prier Jusqu'a Remporter La Victoire
11. Prieres Violentes Pour Humilier Les Problsmes Opiniatres
12. Priere Pour Detruire Les Maladies Et Les Infirmites
13. Le Combat Spirituel Et Le Foyer
14. Bilan Spirituel Personnel
15. Victoires Sur Les Reves Sataniques
16. Prieres De Combat Contre 70 Esprits Dechalnes
17. La Deviation Satanique De La Race Noire
18. Ton Combat Et Ta Strategie

OTHER PUBLICATIONS BY DR. D. K. OLUKOYA

19. Votre Fondement Et Votre Destin
20. Revoquer Les Decrets Malefiques
21. Cantique Des Coritiques
22. Le Mauvais Cri Des Idoles
23. Quand Les Choses Deviennent Difficiles
24. Les Strategies De Prieres Pour Les Celibataires
25. Se Liberer Des Alliances Malefiques
26. Demanteler La Sorcellerie
27. La Deliverance: Le Flacon De Medicament De Dieu
28. La Deliverance De La Tete
29. Commander Le Matin
30. Ne Grand Mais Lie
31. Pouvoir Contre Les Demons Tropicaux
32. Le Programme De Tranfert Des Richesse
33. Les Etudiants A l'ecole De La Peur
34. L'etoile Dans Votre Ciel
35. Les Saisons De La Vie
36. Femme Tu Es Liberee

OTHER PUBLICATIONS BY PASTOR(MRS) SHADE OLUKOYA

1. Power to Fulfil Your Destiny
2. Principles of A Successful Marriage
3. The Call of God
4. The Daughters of Phillip
5. Violence Against Negative Voices
6. Woman of Wonder
7. When Your Destiny is Under Attack
8. I decree an uncommon change

ALL OBTAINABLE AT:

The Battle Cry Christian Ministries-
322, Herbert Macaulay Street, Sabo, Yaba.
P. O. Box 12272, Ikeja, Lagos
Telephone: 08033044239, 01-8044415

MFM International Bookshop
13, Olasimbo Street, Onike-Yaba, Lagos

All MFM Church Branches nationwide
and leading Christian Bookstores

Battle Cry Christian Ministries
Abuja Zonal Office and Bookshop
4, Nasarawa Street, Block A, Shop 4, Garki Old Market.
Phone: 08135865868, 08159103039

BOOK ORDER

Is there any book by
Dr. D. K. Olukoya
(General Overseer MFM Ministries)
that you would like to have?

Have you seen his latest books?
To place an order for this End-Time Materials,
Call: 08161229775

Battle Cry Ministries... *Equipping the saints of God.*

God bless.

www.ingramcontent.com/pod-product-compliance
Lightning Source LLC
Chambersburg PA
CBHW061249040426
42444CB00010B/2319